Original title:

Silent Quest

Author: Sara Säde

ISBN HARDBACK: 978-1-80561-047-2

ISBN PAPERBACK: 978-1-80561-608-5

Wings of the Unseen

In shadows deep where secrets lie,
The whispers of the night birds sigh.
With gentle grace they soar and glide,
On wings of hope, they do not hide.

They chase the stars, a silver dream,
In moonlit beams, they softly beam.
A dance of light where darkness dwells,
In silent tales the heart compels.

Through whispered winds and hidden streams,
They carry forth our quiet dreams.
With every beat, they break the chains,
In vast unknowns, freedom reigns.

Their journey leads to distant shores,
Where courage calls and spirit soars.
In unity, they find their song,
Together brave, where they belong.

So lift your eyes and feel the air,
Embrace the flight, let go of care.
For in the night, the unseen wings,
Will guide us through, and hope still sings.

Portrait of the Unvoiced

In silence, shadows dance and sway,
Each tear unshed, a word to say.
Where dreams reside in muted tones,
The heart speaks loud, yet no one knows.

A canvas stretched, emotions bleed,
In colors dark, a hidden creed.
The whispers lost amidst the dust,
A soul confined, but yearns to trust.

Behind the gaze, a world concealed,
A fortress built, yet unrevealed.
Through veils of doubt, the hope might strain,
To find a voice in all the pain.

Yet from the depths, a spark may rise,
Illuminating darkened skies.
With strokes of light, the truth can bloom,
A portrait formed amidst the gloom.

So let the unvoiced find their ground,
In every silence, beauty's found.
With patience, art will start to flow,
Let every whisper start to glow.

The Shadow Beneath the Surface

Beneath the calm, the waters churn,
Mysteries weave, the depths discern.
A world of silence, secrets kept,
Where shadows linger, thoughts inept.

The moon's soft light, a fleeting guise,
Reflects the truth from unseen eyes.
In whispered sighs, the stories blend,
Each wave a tale, each ripple, a friend.

Yet fear resides in what's concealed,
The heartache penned, the wounds revealed.
In every shadow, specters play,
A dance of doubts that won't decay.

But deep below, in darkest night,
A flicker glows, a chance for light.
From depths unknown, a voice will call,
To cast away the fear of fall.

So seek the truth where shadows roam,
In every heart, a place called home.
The surface glimmers, but depths embrace,
The shadowed truths we must all face.

Whispers of the Soul

In quiet corners, whispers weave,
Soft melodies of those who grieve.
With every breath, a story told,
Of love once warm, now growing cold.

The gentle sigh of time's embrace,
Carves tender lines upon the face.
In every heartbeat, echoes merge,
The soul's sweet song, an endless surge.

Through veils of dreams, the spirits fly,
Their laughter mingling with a sigh.
In shadowed halls where memories dwell,
Each whispering ghost has tales to tell.

Yet within the quiet, strength is found,
A flicker strong, a love profound.
The whispers rise in radiant glow,
A symphony of hearts that know.

So hold the whispers close and dear,
They softly speak of hope and fear.
In every note, a life embraced,
A journey shared, a bond interlaced.

Echoes in the Distance

In twilight's glow, the echoes soar,
A haunting sound from days of yore.
Across the hills, through valleys wide,
The memories walk, where dreams abide.

With every step, the past awakes,
In whispered tones, the silence breaks.
A dance of shadows, tales unfold,
Of love embraced, of hearts consoled.

The winds carry voices, soft and clear,
Each echo speaks of those held dear.
In distant lands, their laughter shared,
In every heart, the love declared.

Yet fleeting is the light we chase,
For echoes fade, but leave their trace.
A gentle linger, a nudge of fate,
In every heartbeat, we relate.

So listen close to what remains,
In echoes soft, a truth sustains.
Through distance far, the love endures,
A timeless bond, forever yours.

Between the Lines of Silence

In whispers soft, the night unfolds,
A world unseen, where secrets rest.
The shadows dance, the stories told,
In quiet hearts, they know the best.

Words linger like a gentle breeze,
A hush of thoughts, unspoken dreams.
Between the lines, the mind finds ease,
In silence deep, or so it seems.

A pulse of truth in muted tones,
The stillness guides the seeker near.
Where echoes cling to quiet stones,
Each breath a note, so crystal clear.

In twilight's grace, connections bloom,
Among the stars, the thoughts entwine.
An inner light dispels the gloom,
Between the lines, our hearts combine.

Quest for Inner Echoes

Beneath the surface, shadows creep,
Where echoes of the past reside.
In gentle waves, my thoughts run deep,
A journey fierce, where dreams collide.

With every step, the echoes call,
Resounding truths I long to find.
Within the silence, I feel small,
Yet brave enough, I seek the mind.

Fragments of hope drift in the air,
Like feathers lost upon the sea.
A quest unfolds, a silent prayer,
To capture whispers meant for me.

As night descends, reflections spark,
In stillness, I embrace the light.
Each echo guides me through the dark,
A faithful map; my heart takes flight.

The Hidden Voyage

A ship awaits beneath the stars,
Sails unfurled, the winds are bold.
Through realms unknown, through light and scars,
The heart embarks, yet untold.

With every wave, the story grows,
A tale of fate, of loss, and gain.
In depths unseen, adventure flows,
Each current whispers through the pain.

A compass set on dreams and hope,
The stars above, a guiding glow.
Across the vast, we learn to cope,
In hidden paths, our spirits flow.

As shadows play on oceans wide,
The voyage calls, we mustn't fear.
For in the depths, our truths abide,
In every swell, the heart draws near.

Still Waters Run Deep

In tranquil lakes where silence sways,
The stillness holds a world within.
Reflections dance in gentle rays,
A secret life where dreams begin.

Beneath the calm, the currents stir,
A depth profound, a silent call.
In whispered tides, our thoughts confer,
Awake the echoes of it all.

The ripples tell of tales once told,
Of hearts that yearn and passions bold.
In stillness found, the truth unfolds,
As shadows grace the waters' hold.

We dip our toes in quiet pools,
Where nature sings of life's embrace.
Amongst the peace, we find the rules,
Of love, of hope, in time and space.

The Unvoiced Journey

Whispers travel through the night,
Unseen paths in soft moonlight.
Hearts carry dreams without a sound,
In silence, the lost voices are found.

Stars above guide the way clear,
Through shadows, we hide every fear.
Each step forward, a tale untold,
In the journey, our souls unfold.

The winds carry secrets anew,
Murmurs of places we never knew.
In the stillness, we find our grace,
An unvoiced journey through time and space.

Paths intertwine where souls collide,
With every heartbeat, we just ride.
A canvas painted in shades of night,
Together we walk, lost in the light.

Muffled Footprints

In the soft earth, stories lie,
Muffled footprints, no goodbye.
Every step a silent quest,
Echoes of hearts seeking rest.

The morning dew hides our trail,
Skies above, vast and pale.
Winds whisper secrets of the day,
In the shadows, we drift and sway.

Leaves fall down with a gentle sigh,
In the twilight, we learn to fly.
Steps remembered in the dark,
Muffled footfalls leave their mark.

As dusk descends, we pause and breathe,
Nature wraps us, we believe.
Every grain of sand, a story told,
In the silence, our spirits unfold.

Reverie in the Dark

When night blankets the skies above,
Dreams awaken, whispering love.
In shadows deep, thoughts entwine,
A reverie in the dark, divine.

Stars flicker like distant thoughts,
In stillness, the universe is sought.
Each heartbeat a soft, guiding spark,
We drift further into the dark.

Thoughts waltz like leaves in the breeze,
Embracing the night, our minds find ease.
Within this silence, we dance and sway,
A reverie in endless play.

The world fades, and time stands still,
Lost in dreams, we learn to thrill.
Together we weave through the night's embrace,
In this darkness, we find our place.

The Sound of Solitude

In the quiet, a voice is born,
A melody of hearts, forlorn.
Whispers linger, fade, then rise,
The sound of solitude softly sighs.

Alone, yet never truly lost,
In silence, we learn the cost.
Every thought a quiet refrain,
The sound of solitude, a sweet pain.

Moments stolen, softly felt,
In shadows, our fears are dealt.
Each heartbeat echoes through the void,
The sound of solitude, unalloyed.

Together apart, we understand,
In loneliness, we find the hand.
Through empty spaces, we paint our dreams,
The sound of solitude, or so it seems.

Whispers in the Void

In shadows deep, where silence sways,
A breath of night, the world decays.
Secrets hum in twilight's haze,
As stars align in whispered ways.

Echoes dance in cosmic tune,
Veils of fate and dreams attune.
Silent calls on wings of rune,
The heart beats soft, a gentle boon.

Lost in space, the soul takes flight,
Guided by the pale moonlight.
In the dark, there's pure insight,
A soothing balm, a tranquil sight.

From depths unknown, the silence grows,
Cradled in a cosmic prose.
Wonders dwell where no one knows,
In whispers born, a stillness flows.

Echoes of the Unseen

Across the long and winding road,
Mysteries speak, a hidden code.
In the breeze, lost tales bestowed,
Embrace the shadows, light erode.

Murmurs linger, soft and light,
Fading echoes in the night.
Each step taken feels so right,
Guided by the spirit's sight.

Awake to worlds that intertwine,
Glimpse the threads that softly shine.
Every heartbeat feels divine,
In spaces where the heart aligns.

Waves of thoughts that rise and fall,
Listening close, to nature's call.
In silence, hear the universe's thrall,
As love and wisdom weave it all.

The Journey Within

Paths untraveled, dreams unfurled,
In stillness rests a vibrant world.
With open heart, the steps revealed,
The soul's own truth is gently healed.

Wander forth through forests pale,
Where whispers tell a deeper tale.
Every sigh, a sacred trail,
In harmony, we will prevail.

Through valleys deep and mountains high,
Beneath the vast and open sky.
In each moment, learning why,
The inner voice will never lie.

Reflections dance on waters clear,
Bearing wisdom, kind and near.
In every joy, in every tear,
The journey's gift is always here.

Embrace of Stillness

In quietude, a gentle grace,
The world slows down, finds its place.
Breath in sync with nature's pace,
In soft embrace, all fears efface.

Beneath the trees, in shadows cast,
Moments linger, memories vast.
Time unwinds, both slow and fast,
In stillness found, a peace amassed.

Where whispers dance, in tranquility,
The heart unlocks, finds purity.
Through endless night, through every spree,
In break of dawn, we truly see.

Trust the silence, embrace the now,
With open hearts, we take a vow.
To cherish time, to live somehow,
In each breath drawn, we learn to bow.

The Path Less Mentioned

In shadows deep where few have tread,
A whisper calls, soft as a thread.
Footsteps linger on unmarked sand,
A journey waits, not always planned.

Winds of change beckon in the night,
Stars guide the way with gentle light.
Exploring paths that twist and turn,
In every step, there's more to learn.

The heart beats strong, a steady drum,
Through tangled vines where few will come.
Embrace the wild, the strange, the new,
Adventure starts with the brave and true.

With every stumble, grace appears,
Forget the doubts, forget the fears.
The road unfolds, revealing grace,
A dance of fate in timeless space.

So tread the lines that none have drawn,
A symphony at the break of dawn.
For every road less taken leads,
To awaken souls and hidden seeds.

Finding Clarity in the Void

In silence deep where echoes fade,
A stillness sings, a serenade.
Lost in the vastness, eyes upraised,
In darkness, light is often praised.

Thoughts like clouds drift and align,
Floating softly, pure, divine.
In the void, the heart's song flows,
Unraveled dreams begin to glow.

With every breath, the chaos clears,
The mind awakens, sheds its fears.
In the emptiness, a bright spark,
Illuminates the silent dark.

Moments linger, timeless, still,
In the deep hush, the soul can build.
Finding clarity, the heart's delight,
In the soft embrace of the night.

From the void springs a vibrant hue,
A canvas fresh, a world anew.
In finding self, we find our way,
The light within, the break of day.

Beneath the Surface of Tranquility

A still lake reflects the sky,
Whispers of peace, as time slips by.
Ripples dance on the water's face,
Where dreams awaken in gentle space.

Beneath the calm, a world does swirl,
Secrets unfurl, like a tender pearl.
In depths unknown, the currents sway,
Carrying thoughts that drift away.

The quiet hum of life below,
Echoes softly, a hidden flow.
In tranquility, chaos might hide,
Beneath the surface, a restless tide.

Roots entwine in the earth's embrace,
Branches reach high, seeking grace.
Nature's whispers, a soothing balm,
In the heart of peace, the world feels calm.

To dive deeper, seek what's true,
There's strength in silence, known to few.
Beneath the surface, life sustains,
A symphony of sweet refrains.

In the Realm of Quiet Reveries

In twilight shades where dreams reside,
Thoughts gently flow, like a quiet tide.
Whispers weave through the evening air,
A realm of wonders, beyond compare.

Stars sprinkle thoughts across the night,
Painting visions in silver light.
In the stillness, the soul takes flight,
Into the depths, where hearts feel right.

Memories dance in soft repose,
In the corners where the stillness grows.
Lost in time, the moments blend,
Where dreams begin and never end.

Within this space, the mind's a stream,
Flowing freely, crafting a dream.
In every thought, a story hints,
A tapestry that silence prints.

In quiet reveries, find your peace,
Where worries fade and tensions cease.
In this realm, let your spirit soar,
Embrace the magic forevermore.

Navigating the Uncharted Depths

In shadows deep, where dreams reside,
A compass lost, yet hearts abide.
The currents pull, both fierce and grand,
We sail to find a distant land.

With every wave, a story told,
Of battles fought and treasures old.
The stars above, our guiding light,
In darkest nights, they shine so bright.

Through storm and calm, we seek the truth,
In whispered winds and cries of youth.
The depths we dive, the heights we scale,
In quest of love, we shall not fail.

As waters churn, the heart does yearn,
With passion's flame, the fire will burn.
Each tide may rise, each ebb may fall,
But in this dance, we hear love's call.

So set your sails, embrace the course,
For out of fear, we find our source.
In uncharted depths, hearts intertwine,
In every loss, a chance to shine.

Essence of the Unspoken

In silence deep, a language flows,
Where words fall short, true feeling grows.
The glance, a whisper, the touch, a sigh,
In stillness, secrets learn to fly.

A breath between, a heart's intent,
In unmarked paths, our spirits vent.
With eyes that speak, and souls that blend,
We find the forms of hearts that mend.

Though voices may fade, the truth prevails,
In every pulse, our love exails.
The unlit spaces where shadows play,
In essence found, we find our way.

As night descends, we draw so near,
In quietude, we shed our fear.
Unspoken thoughts, like stars align,
In the abyss, our dreams entwine.

Let words dissolve, in whispers soft,
In silent realms, we drift aloft.
For what we hold, beyond the sound,
Is where true essence can be found.

Solace in the Stillness

In gentle hush, the world does cease,
Where chaos fades, we find our peace.
Amidst the noise, a quiet grace,
In stillness, we discover space.

The heartbeats slow, the joys unfold,
In moments soft, our truths are told.
With every breath, a mindful trace,
We seek the warmth of our embrace.

The world external may fight and scream,
But in the still, we weave our dream.
A lullaby that softly plays,
In tranquil light, our spirits raise.

While shadows dance, we softly sway,
The night unfolds, we drift away.
In timeless realms, our souls take flight,
In solace found, we chase the light.

So lean into the calm, unwind,
In gentle whispers, love we find.
In every pause, a chance to grow,
In stillness sweet, our hearts will glow.

Reflections of the Soul

In mirrored depths, the heart reveals,
Our whispered truths, the spirit feels.
Each glance a story, each sigh a song,
In the ebb and flow, we all belong.

Through shifting sands, our shadows weave,
In fleeting moments, learn to believe.
A dance of light, a fleeting grace,
In every tear, we find our place.

The canvas bare, we paint our dreams,
In colors bright, our journey beams.
With every stroke, our essence grows,
In every trial, the spirit knows.

The echoes soft, of love's embrace,
In every heartbeat, find your pace.
Reflections deep, a timeless scroll,
In every glance, we touch the soul.

So gaze within, embrace the hue,
For in the light, love's depth shines through.
In reflections pure, our hearts unite,
In every shadow, we find the light.

Chasing Shadows

In the quiet of the night,
I wander through the mist.
Figures dance with fleeting light,
Dreams that can't be kissed.

Whispers call from distant shores,
Echoes of forgotten dreams.
Through the dark, my spirit soars,
Nothing's ever what it seems.

Every step, a pulse of fear,
As shadows stretch and grow.
I chase the things I hold so near,
Yet find they do not glow.

With the moon, I spin and twirl,
Embracing all the unknown.
Chasing shadows in a whirl,
In this world, I'm not alone.

But dawn will break, the chase must end,
And shadows fade away.
In the light, my heart can mend,
To live another day.

Threads of the Unseen

Tangled webs of silent fear,
Woven in the dark of night.
Secrets whispered, never clear,
Holding truths that pierce the light.

Every thread a silent sigh,
Binding stories, dreams unsaid.
In the chaos, sparks will fly,
Emotions dance, a whispered dread.

Unraveling, the heart will seek,
Questions borne on fragile breath.
In the shadows, spirits speak,
Chasing life beyond the death.

Hopes entwined, they rise and fall,
Fleeting glimpses of the whole.
In this tapestry, we crawl,
Finding solace for the soul.

Yet still we weave, with trembling hands,
The fabric of what binds.
In the silence, hope still stands,
Threads of love, hearts intertwined.

Midnight Musings

As the stars begin to glow,
Thoughts drift on a silver stream.
In the quiet, whispers flow,
Cradling each forgotten dream.

Midnight casts its shadow deep,
On the canvas of the mind.
Thoughts awaken from their sleep,
In the darkness, truths unwind.

Questions linger in the air,
As time slows to a gentle hum.
Every worry laid bare,
With the dawn, the answers come.

In the stillness, fears take flight,
Fleeting glimpses of what's real.
Lessons learned in the soft night,
Moments captured that we feel.

With the first light, we'll unfold,
Pieces of our midnight tales.
In the day, we'll be more bold,
Navigating life's vast trails.

Confessions of the Unexpressed

Deep within, a tempest brews,
Words unspoken, weight of shame.
Silent cries, the heart renews,
Fear of love, a burning flame.

In the shadows, feelings hide,
Yearning souls on fragile ground.
Barriers rise, we turn and bide,
Echoes lost, we seek, we're found.

Every glance, a story told,
Yet lips are sealed, hearts in chains.
In the quiet, passions bold,
Feelings drown in silent strains.

Will we ever find our voice?
Speak the truth that lies within?
Or by silence, we'll rejoice,
Wondering where love's been?

Confessions linger like the night,
Hanging on the edge of air.
In the dawn, we search for light,
To express the love we share.

A Canvas of Quiet

In the hush of the morn light,
Whispers dance on the breeze.
Colors blend soft and bright,
Stillness paints with ease.

Each leaf holds a secret,
As shadows stretch and yawn.
The world takes a deep breath,
Awakening at dawn.

Gentle waves kiss the shore,
With a silent, soothing sound.
Nature's heart beats with lore,
In this tranquil ground.

Among the rustling trees,
Time pauses to reflect.
Moments flow like the seas,
In quiet, we connect.

As day unfolds its grace,
The canvas of stillness gleams.
In this sacred space,
Life whispers through our dreams.

The Uncharted Terrain

Footsteps lead to the unknown,
Where paths are yet to form.
In wild beauty, we're shown,
The thrill of a new storm.

Mountains rise like giants,
Clouds whisper tales of old.
Each peak, a brave defiance,
In their majesty, bold.

Rivers carve through the land,
Painting stories untold.
With courage, we stand,
As adventures unfold.

The air is rich with promise,
Every turn reveals more.
In the heart of this abyss,
We'll find what we explore.

With each step, seeds are sown,
Hope grows in the wild.
In this place, we are shown,
The joy of the unstyled.

A Journey Through Still Waters

In mirrored depths, we drift,
Reflections of the sky.
Gentle ripples, a soft gift,
Sailing dreams that fly.

The sun dips low, a warm glow,
As evening starts to blend.
With every paddle's slow flow,
We find a deeper friend.

Whispers of the water call,
In harmony, we glide.
Nature's peace surrounds us all,
With every tranquil tide.

Stars awaken, the night sighs,
Embracing what was found.
In the quiet, our heart flies,
In stillness, we are bound.

Together, we chart our course,
Through shadows and through light.
In this journey, a soft force,
Guides us through the night.

In the Embrace of Dusk

As day surrenders to night,
Colors fade, shadows blend.
In the stillness, feels right,
Where the edges transcend.

Crickets sing their soft song,
A lullaby of rest.
In the fading light, we belong,
Where the world feels blessed.

Stars emerge like soft sparks,
Winking from velvet skies.
In the quiet, our hearts embark,
On journeys that arise.

Wrapped in twilight's embrace,
The magic slowly swells.
In this serene, sacred space,
Every shadow tells.

Beneath the moon's soft glow,
Hope flickers and expands.
In the dusk, we learn to grow,
Guided by gentle hands.

Footsteps in the Silence

In the hush of twilight's grace,
Footsteps whisper, trace the space.
Echoes linger, soft and light,
Guiding souls into the night.

Stars awaken, fade the gloom,
Their gentle light dispels the doom.
Through the silence, secrets flow,
Carrying dreams that softly glow.

A path unwinds beneath the moon,
Each step a song, a timeless tune.
Silent wishes in the air,
Hopes entwined, beyond despair.

When footsteps fade and shadows blend,
A journey starts, no end to tend.
In the quiet, hearts align,
Finding solace, pure, divine.

Threads of Hidden Dreams

In a tapestry of quiet night,
Threads of dreams weave soft and bright.
Whispers linger, tales unfold,
Stories waiting to be told.

Colors dance beneath the seams,
Stories echo, lost in dreams.
Every thread a wish once spun,
Hopes entwined, a race begun.

Through the fabric, time flows slow,
In its pattern, hidden glow.
Threads entwined in shadows' play,
Guiding hearts, come what may.

As dawn approaches, dreams may drift,
Yet in silence, they still lift.
Every heartbeat, every seam,
Holds the essence of a dream.

Beneath the Quiet

Beneath the quiet, secrets sigh,
In the stillness, echoes fly.
Thoughts like whispers, softly speak,
In the corners, truths we seek.

The moonlight spills on ancient stone,
Where memories linger, softly grown.
Shadows stretch, with tales to share,
In the silence, we lay bare.

Every breath a silent prayer,
Every heartbeat, pure and rare.
In the chaos, find the peace,
Where dreams and quiet thoughts release.

Beneath the quiet, hearts unbind,
In the solace, worlds aligned.
Time unfolds, a gentle guide,
Leading us to where we hide.

In the Company of Shadows

In the company of shadows cast,
Silent figures roam the past.
Dancing lightly on the wall,
Echoes of a distant call.

Whispers linger in the night,
Soft and fleeting, out of sight.
Hands outstretched, they reach and sway,
Maps of dreams that fade away.

Underneath the silver glow,
Shadowed paths begin to flow.
Hearts entwined in quiet grace,
Find the courage to embrace.

In their presence, fears dissolve,
Mysteries that all resolve.
In the company of shadows near,
Every heartbeat, sharp and clear.

Whispers of the Unseen

In shadows deep, they softly tread,
Voices linger where light has fled.
Secrets weave in silence spun,
A tale of two, yet told by one.

Through veils of mist, they call my name,
Flickering whispers, never the same.
A dance of echoes, mysterious art,
Unseen specters that touch the heart.

They float like feathers on a breeze,
Carrying thoughts that aim to please.
Hidden dreams in twilight entrust,
To silent watchers, in them we trust.

In quiet corners, truths reside,
Nurtured softly, fear set aside.
Winds murmur secrets, lost and found,
In every heartbeat, their sound profound.

In shadows, belief takes flight,
As whispers of unseen ignite the night.
Though obscured, they spin the tale,
Of life's journey, where we prevail.

Echoes Beneath the Stars

Under the canopy, stars gleam bright,
Echoes of wishes on a velvet night.
Softly they shimmer, dreams take flight,
Guided by hope, hearts alight.

Among the constellations, stories stir,
Ancient voices of what once were.
Past and present, an intertwining thread,
In the silence, all is said.

Night air laced with mysteries deep,
Promises whispered, secrets to keep.
Beneath the vault where shadows play,
Yearning souls wander and sway.

With every heartbeat, the stars respond,
Bridging the gaps of beyond and bond.
A tapestry woven with golden grace,
Echoes of longing, a timeless embrace.

In the stillness where silence thrives,
The universe dances, and love survives.
Together we gaze, our spirits free,
In echoes beneath, eternity.

The Sound of Stillness

In the quiet, time stands still,
A gentle whisper, nature's thrill.
The rustle of leaves, a soft caress,
In stillness found, there's no distress.

The world retreats, a gentle sigh,
Moments linger, as dreams pass by.
In tranquil spaces, shadows blend,
Every heartbeat, a calming friend.

Beneath the surface, where silence reigns,
The murmur of thoughts, unspent gains.
Tides of emotion ebb and flow,
In stillness, seeds of wisdom grow.

Listen closely; let echoes arise,
The sound of stillness is a prized surprise.
In the absence of noise, clarity beams,
A symphony woven from quiet dreams.

In the hush, we find our way,
Navigating through night and day.
Embracing the peace, our spirits soar,
In the sound of stillness, forevermore.

Veil of Forgotten Dreams

Behind the veil, shadows dance,
Whispers of hope, a fleeting chance.
Forgotten dreams in twilight's hue,
Waiting for hearts to break through.

Memories linger, like morning mist,
Soft echoes of what we resist.
In the stillness, they call our name,
Rekindling the spark, igniting the flame.

The past holds treasures, lost and found,
In whispering winds, their voices sound.
Beneath the surface, a story we weave,
In forgotten dreams, we dare to believe.

Through layers of time, we tread the line,
Mapping our journey in intricate design.
Each dream a thread that colors our days,
In the fabric of life, we find our ways.

So lift the veil, let visions soar,
Embrace the dreams that we once bore.
For in each heartbeat, a promise gleams,
Life's tapestry woven from forgotten dreams.

Beyond Words

In whispers soft, we find our truth,
Unspoken love in fleeting youth.
A glance exchanged, no need for sound,
In silence deep, our dreams abound.

The echoes fade, yet still we know,
Our hearts entwined, forever flow.
Beyond the page, where stories blend,
In silent vows, our souls ascend.

Through tangled thoughts and shadows cast,
The moments shared, forever last.
In every sigh, a world unchained,
In stillness found, our hearts remain.

With every beat, a tale unfolds,
In quiet light, our fate foretold.
Beyond the words, our spirits soar,
A language pure, forevermore.

So let us dance where echoes fade,
In realms of dreams, our feelings laid.
Beyond the words, through time we glide,
In every heartbeat, we confide.

Harmonies of the Invisible

In shadows dark, a melody plays,
Invisible chords in twilight's haze.
Life's symphony, a soft refrain,
In whispered notes, we feel the pain.

The stars align in silent queues,
A cosmic dance that we must choose.
In every breath, a harmony,
Invisible threads bind you and me.

With every tear, a chord is struck,
A song of hope, when times are tough.
In hidden realms, where spirits roam,
We find our way, we find our home.

Upon the winds, the secrets glide,
In every heart, they safely hide.
Through unseen paths, our spirits flow,
A tapestry of what we know.

Together we weave, in love's embrace,
Harmonies that time can't erase.
In whispers soft, our souls align,
In the invisible, love's light will shine.

The Still Heart

In quietude, the heart does dwell,
A sanctuary, where dreams swell.
With every pause, a moment stays,
In stillness deep, the spirit plays.

Beneath the noise, a pulse resides,
Where time slows down, and truth abides.
In gentle beats, the world retreats,
The calm within, where life repeats.

Each breath a gift, each sigh a song,
In silence found, where we belong.
With every thought, the shadows fade,
In peace profound, our fears cascade.

Through open skies and starlit nights,
The still heart finds its endless lights.
In tranquil realms, our souls unite,
With every beat, we take our flight.

So let us treasure every pause,
In stillness found, we find our cause.
The still heart speaks, in tender tones,
In quiet love, we find our homes.

Labyrinth of the Mind

In winding paths, the thoughts align,
A maze of dreams where shadows twine.
Each turn a whisper, secrets hold,
In labyrinthine tales, truth unfolds.

Through corridors of hope and fear,
The echoes linger, crystal clear.
In every corner, doubts reside,
Yet in the twists, our joys abide.

With every choice, a new route drawn,
In tangled webs, the light is gone.
Yet through the haze, a spark appears,
In labyrinth's depth, we face our fears.

Each step we take, a journey vast,
Through memories shared and spells we've cast.
In winding ways, we'll find our way,
In labyrinth of thoughts, we sway.

So dare to roam, through night and day,
In minds' embrace, we'll find the way.
The labyrinth shifts, but we explore,
Within our hearts, forevermore.

Solo Dances of the Heart

In shadows deep, a movement starts,
A whisper drifts, it sings in parts.
A solo dance beneath the moon,
Where silent echoes find their tune.

With every step, a breath of peace,
In solitude, the worries cease.
A melody within the soul,
Each twirl a story, making whole.

The heart, a stage of grace and fire,
In every beat, a fierce desire.
The rhythm flows like water's stream,
In silent moments, we can dream.

As stars align, the night unfolds,
In whispered winds, the heart beholds.
The gentle sway, a sweet embrace,
In solo dances, we find our place.

So let the music grace the night,
In every step, we find our light.
The heart's own dance, a sacred art,
A journey deep, a work of heart.

The Invisible Expedition

Beneath the veil of everyday,
An unseen path leads us away.
Through whispered winds and hidden trails,
A quest unfolds where magic sails.

With every heartbeat, secrets flow,
The map is drawn by dreams we know.
Each step a story, lost in time,
In silence found, our souls will climb.

We wander realms of thought and light,
In shadows cast, we find our sight.
The invisible, a guiding star,
With every breath, we travel far.

In echoes soft, the past remains,
In whispered woods, a truth retains.
An odyssey, though not in view,
The heart speaks loud; it knows what's true.

So take a chance, let spirit roam,
In the unknown, we find a home.
This invisible quest, though obscure,
Is where the heart and dreams endure.

The Secrets We Carry

In quiet corners, secrets dwell,
Within our hearts, a whispered spell.
Burdened thoughts, like shadows near,
Each hidden truth, a trace of fear.

We walk the line of joy and pain,
Beneath the smiles, we feel the strain.
With every pulse, a tale unfolds,
The weight of wishes, silence holds.

The stories told with eyes that gleam,
In moments shared, we dare to dream.
Each secret weave, a fabric worn,
In connections made, we are reborn.

Yet in the dark, we find the light,
The hidden gems that shine so bright.
With trust, we share, reveal our core,
The secrets fade, we learn to soar.

So in this life, embrace the scars,
The truths unearthed, like guiding stars.
For all the secrets that we bear,
Are threads of love in life's great care.

Silent Revelations

In quiet dawn, the world awakes,
A stillness found, the heart remakes.
Within the silence, truths collide,
In space unfilled, our thoughts reside.

The whispers soft, like morning rain,
In gentle rhythms, heal the pain.
Through veils of doubt, the light breaks through,
In silent moments, we find the new.

Each revelation, like a spark,
Illuminates the endless dark.
The soul knows well, though words are few,
In stillness lies what feels most true.

So listen close to what's inside,
In silent realms, our dreams confide.
With every breath, a story spun,
Through quiet spaces, we become one.

Embrace the silence, let it soar,
In the unknown, we find our core.
These silent revelations, deep and wide,
Unravel worlds where hearts reside.

Shadows of the Unspoken Desire

In the dim light, whispers breathe,
Silent hearts, the truths they weave.
Longing glimmers in the dark,
Yearning dances, leaving a mark.

Fingers brush against the veil,
Hidden emotions start to sail.
Unsaid words, a heavy weight,
In shadows deep, they quietly wait.

Eyes that speak when mouths are still,
In quiet moments, they fulfill.
The heart's echo, a secret song,
In the silence, where we belong.

Dreams flicker like candlelight,
Softly guiding through the night.
A path woven through desire,
In the dark, our souls conspire.

With every beat, a truth unfolds,
In shadows, the longing holds.
An unspoken dance, a lover's game,
In silence, we're always the same.

The Quest for Inner Peace

In a world that spins so fast,
I seek the stillness, my anchor cast,
Amidst the noise, a gentle hum,
The heartbeat of where I come from.

Leaves whisper secrets to the breeze,
Nature's symphony puts my mind at ease.
In tranquil moments, I find my ground,
In every sigh, a solace profound.

Meditation's embrace, a tender grace,
With each breath, I reclaim my place.
Waves of calm wash over me,
In the quiet, I'm truly free.

Mountains stand tall, embracing the sky,
Reminding me how to rise high.
In the depths of silence, I hear my soul,
In the stillness, I become whole.

With every step, I tread with care,
Finding peace in the thin air.
The quest continues, my heart aligned,
To inner peace, my spirit refined.

Secrets in the Still Air

In the hush of dusk, secrets breathe,
Floating softly like autumn leaves.
Stories untold linger near,
In the stillness, they appear.

The moon whispers truths so bright,
Casting shadows in the night.
With every star, a dream takes flight,
In the quiet, we find our light.

Winds caress with gentle hands,
Guiding us to forgotten lands.
Where silence wraps around the heart,
In still air, we play our part.

Echoes of laughter fill the space,
Memories linger, a warm embrace.
In every breath, a tale unwinds,
In the stillness, serenity finds.

Like whispers soft within the night,
Hidden gems flicker and ignite.
In the still air, secrets stay,
Calling softly, come what may.

Between the Lines of Calm

In the spaces where silence dwells,
A quiet peace, the spirit swells.
Between the lines of what is known,
Gentle truths begin to be shown.

Moments linger like a soft sigh,
Underneath the vast, open sky.
The whispers of the heart provide,
A gentle guide, where dreams reside.

Each breath a promise, serene and clear,
In this stillness, there's nothing to fear.
The world outside fades further away,
Between the lines, I choose to stay.

Harmony flows like a quiet stream,
In its embrace, I find my dream.
With every heartbeat, rhythm gifts,
In calm's cradle, the soul uplifts.

Connected deeply to the unseen,
In tranquil moments, I am keen.
Between life's lines, in the space they carve,
I find the peace for which I starve.

A Dance with the Void

In shadows deep where silence sways,
The echoes of forgotten days.
A waltz with darkness, hearts collide,
In twilight's grip, we dare confide.

Whispers weave through empty space,
A fleeting breath, a ghostly trace.
Each step we take, a question posed,
In the abyss, our truth exposed.

Stars ignite like sparks of hope,
As we on fragile dreams elope.
With every twirl, the cosmos spins,
In this vast void, our dance begins.

Yet fear and doubt creep close behind,
A haunting tune that's intertwined.
We find our rhythm, lose our way,
In this dark dance, we choose to stay.

The silence swells, the night is bold,
In shadows deep, our hearts unfold.
Together here, let spirits soar,
In the embrace of the void, explore.

Wandering Thoughts

Drifting gently through the mind,
A tapestry of thoughts entwined.
Like leaves that dance on autumn breeze,
In random moments, we find ease.

What lies beyond the fleeting dreams?
A world that's stitched with silent seams.
Each memory a thread to weave,
In tangled paths, we learn to believe.

A whisper here, a murmur there,
Ideas flutter in the air.
Conversations with a shadowed ghost,
In wandering thoughts, we find our host.

Curiosity feeds the soul,
In endless search, we find our role.
With every question, more arise,
In the labyrinth, wisdom lies.

With open hearts, we roam the night,
Chasing flickers of borrowed light.
In every turn, the journey brings,
The beauty found in simple things.

Forgotten Corners of the Mind

In the attic of my thoughts, I see,
Whispers of what used to be.
Dusty dreams and faded smiles,
Echo through these empty miles.

A forgotten song plays softly still,
Notes once sharp now gently chill.
In corners dark, the past resides,
Where time and memory confides.

The scent of ages lingers sweet,
As shadows dance on weary feet.
Each fragment holds a story tight,
In twilight's glow, they seek the light.

Unlocking doors to what I've lost,
Rekindling flames at any cost.
Through fragile threads, I navigate,
And find the paths I left to fate.

In silent rooms, the echoes throng,
In these corners, I still belong.
Through faded hues, the truth will show,
Forgotten dreams, alive and aglow.

The Call of Quietude

Beneath the stars, the silence hums,
In tranquil night, the spirit comes.
A gentle whisper, soft and clear,
Inviting souls to linger near.

Time slows down in this embrace,
A serene joy, a sacred space.
The breath of peace, a soothing balm,
In quietude, we find our calm.

The world outside fades into bliss,
In moments still, we find our kiss.
With every heartbeat, echoes grow,
The call of silent truths we know.

The soul retreats, the noise subsides,
In depths of night where stillness hides.
Unraveled thought, a tapestry,
In quietude, we learn to be.

Through gentle echoes, we are led,
In whispered tones, no words are said.
In this pure space, we come alive,
The call of quietude, we thrive.

Seeking the Unseen

In the quiet woods we roam,
Whispers of the lost we seek.
Paths hidden by twilight's cloak,
Dreams linger where shadows speak.

Stars above begin to twinkle,
Guiding us through dusky trails.
Each step draws a curious heart,
Through silence, we hear the veils.

Eyes searching for the unshown,
Truth waits just beyond our grasp.
With every breath, a chance unfolds,
In mystery's tender clasp.

Time falters in this sacred space,
Where echoes of the past reside.
Among the unseen we shall tread,
With courage as our guide.

So let us wander ever far,
In realms where wonder may arise.
For in seeking what's concealed,
We find the beauty of the skies.

Where Shadows Walk

Beneath the veil of moonlit night,
Where mysteries intertwine.
Echoes dance along the walls,
With stories lost in time.

Footsteps tracing silent paths,
Through trees that whisper low.
The heart beats in the darkness,
As secrets ebb and flow.

Stars hang like distant lanterns,
Illuminating fears untold.
Yet shadows hold their own embrace,
In the quiet, dreams unfold.

Mists curl softly 'round our feet,
As visions blend with night.
In this realm where shadows walk,
We seek the inner light.

The world outside sleeps unaware,
While we tread softly here.
In the realms where shadows flow,
We find what we hold dear.

Murmurs of the Night

Stillness wraps the earth in dreams,
As stars begin their dance.
Soft sighs breathe from the shadows,
In night's enchanting trance.

The moon spills silver on the ground,
Each beam a secret ray.
The world beneath its glow breathes deep,
As night turns into day.

Quiet whispers fill the air,
Carried by a gentle breeze.
They weave through branches overhead,
Rustling leaves like soft pleas.

Time moves slowly, yet it flies,
In moments wrapped in peace.
Murmurs of the night call out,
Inviting hearts to cease.

Let us lay among the stars,
Where dreams and silence unite.
In the tapestry of night,
We find our pure delight.

The Beauty of Unknowing

In every step, uncertainty,
A dance on paths unclear.
Yet within this gentle chaos,
Lies the spark we hold dear.

Life blooms in the uncharted,
Where fear meets wild delight.
In questions that remain unasked,
We find new wings in flight.

The world unfolds its stories,
Each moment ripe with chance.
In the art of the unknown,
We learn to love, to dance.

Wonders whisper in the still,
Awakening the soul's call.
In shadows where visions flicker,
We dare to rise, not fall.

So cherish the paths untraveled,
Embrace the unclear view.
For in the beauty of unknowing,
Life's mysteries pull us through.

Traces of Unvoiced Longing

In the shadows where whispers dwell,
Silent echoes bid farewell.
Hearts that yearn, yet never speak,
Fading dreams that seem so weak.

Cloaked in night, the secrets lie,
Beneath the stars, a muted sigh.
Yearning glances cast above,
Seeking warmth, the touch of love.

Faintest trails of words unsaid,
Linger softly, paint the thread.
In the stillness, hearts entwine,
Lost in longing, fervent, divine.

With time's passage, fades the light,
Memories dance in the quiet night.
Unvoiced searches for the true,
Trace the paths that lead to you.

From the depths of bitter sweet,
Longing whispers, soft retreat.
In the space between each heart,
Resides the longing, set apart.

Gaze into the Abyss of Solitude

In the stillness, shadows creep,
Echoes whisper secrets deep.
Gaze into the void so wide,
Where the restless thoughts abide.

Each silence tells a tale unheard,
Isolation's song, so absurd.
Eyes that search for distant shores,
Yearn for peace, yet crave for more.

The mirror fails to find the soul,
Within the depths, we lose control.
Reflections twist in darkened light,
Solitude's dance, a haunting sight.

Fleeting moments, truths confined,
Gaze into the dark, unkind.
But in the quiet, we may find,
The strength within the lonesome mind.

Through the abyss, we journey far,
Chasing dreams, each flickered star.
In the silence, courage grows,
From solitude, the spirit flows.

The Uncharted Silence

In the spaces between each word,
Lies a resonance unheard.
The silence speaks in vibrant hues,
Calling forth the hidden muse.

Vast horizons stretch so wide,
Gentle whispers that abide.
In uncharted realms, we roam,
Seeking solace, finding home.

The quietude, a canvas bare,
Painted dreams fill the air.
Each heartbeat forms a melody,
In this realm of reverie.

Time stands still in silent grace,
Echoes linger, soft embrace.
Through the void, we start to trace,
The beauty found in empty space.

Unraveled thoughts, like stars aglow,
Illuminate where feelings flow.
In this silence, truth ignites,
Guiding hearts to lofty heights.

Murmurs of the Soul

In the depths, a whisper stirs,
A hidden voice beneath the purrs.
Murmurs echo through the haze,
Guiding hearts through winding mazes.

Each sigh, a thread of the divine,
Connecting souls across the line.
An orchestra of muted screams,
Filling voids with unspoken dreams.

Through the cracks, the light will seep,
Bringing forth the truths we keep.
In the stillness, listen close,
For the soul reveals the most.

Every heartbeat tells a tale,
In the whispers, we'll unveil.
Murmurs soft, like morning dew,
Flowing gently, ever true.

Awakening in twilight glow,
Murmurs mark the paths we go.
In the symphony of our grace,
The heartfelt whispers find their place.

In Search of Quietude

In the stillness, whispers dwell,
Nature's breath, a calming spell.
Leaves, they dance in soft embrace,
Lost within this tranquil space.

Dreams ignite in twilight's glow,
A stream of thoughts begins to flow.
Clouds of doubt drift far away,
In this haven, I wish to stay.

Gentle breezes cradle sound,
In the silence, peace is found.
Where the heart learns to align,
In the quiet, I am fine.

Stars above in twinkling grace,
Echoes of a sacred place.
With each breath, I softly sigh,
In search of calm, I learn to fly.

Moments blend, they intertwine,
In stillness, hearts begin to shine.
In this quest, my soul finds rest,
In search of quietude, I'm blessed.

The Journey Within Shadows

Step by step through darkened halls,
Where the silence softly calls.
Footprints echo, softly tread,
Chasing light where shadows spread.

Beneath the veil of hidden fears,
The past unveils its whispered tears.
Ghosts of memories come and go,
In the heart, their stories flow.

As I wander, truth reveals,
Layers hidden, time unveils.
With each shadow, I must face,
The journey leads to a sacred place.

In the depths, I find my light,
Glimmers shining through the night.
Healing whispers guide my way,
In this journey, I will stay.

Through the dark, I long to see,
What the shadows hold for me.
A deeper strength begins to rise,
In this journey, I become wise.

Hushed Footprints on the Path

On the trail where silence reigns,
Hushed footprints tell of hidden gains.
Nature's voice, a mellow hum,
Guides the heart where rhythms come.

Crickets sing in twilight's glow,
While the cool night breezes blow.
Stars are secrets, softly shared,
In the moment, none compared.

Through the forest, shadows dance,
Mysteries tucked in a glance.
Each step taken, wisdom grows,
In this path, the spirit knows.

Echoes of the earth below,
Whisper tales that time shall sow.
In the quiet, souls align,
Hushed footprints speak, they intertwine.

With each journey, life unveils,
Stories spun in tender trails.
In the silence, I connect,
Hushed footprints lead to what I reflect.

Muffled Voices of the Heart

In the corners where dreams reside,
Muffled voices can't be denied.
Whispers soft like gentle rain,
Carrying both love and pain.

Every heartbeat tells a tale,
Of hopes and fears that never pale.
In the stillness, truths emerge,
Muffled voices start to surge.

Yearning deep within my soul,
Fighting shadows, seeking whole.
With each pulse, a secret sigh,
In this echo, I learn to fly.

Gentle hums push through the veil,
Guiding paths where hearts set sail.
Every whisper, a tender art,
Embracing all, the muffled heart.

Through the chaos, find the grace,
Listen closely, heart's embrace.
In the quiet, I discern,
Muffled voices, lessons learned.

Shadows of the Heart

In the twilight where we meet,
Whispers linger, soft and sweet.
A dance of shadows, light entwined,
Echoes of love, so intertwined.

Silhouettes on the wall of time,
Fleeting moments, you and I.
In every beat, the heart will spark,
Illuminating shadows dark.

Memories drift like autumn leaves,
Secrets held, the heart believes.
Through the darkness, we find grace,
In the shadows, love's embrace.

Fading slowly into night,
Yet the heart still holds the light.
Even as the edges blur,
Our shadows speak, no need for words.

Together still, we'll face the dawn,
With every breath, our bond lives on.
In the silence, hearts will chart,
Endless pathways, shadows start.

Unheard Steps

In the quiet of the night,
Footsteps wander without light.
Where the stars refuse to gleam,
Hopes drift softly like a dream.

Beneath the veil of moon's embrace,
An unseen path, a hidden place.
Each step taken, silent plea,
Whispers echo, wild and free.

In the dark, the heart will roam,
Searching always for a home.
In the stillness, time stands still,
Chasing shadows, seeking thrill.

Unheard echoes in the gloom,
Bring forth life where dreams can't bloom.
Every heartbeat marks a trace,
In the vastness, lost in space.

With each breath, we move ahead,
Through the silence, fears we shed.
Unseen paths shall lead us there,
In the quiet, we'll find care.

The Language of Solitude

In the stillness, words unspoken,
Hearts learn language, soft and broken.
Between the lines, a world exists,
Where silence wraps us in its mist.

Alone yet not, in thoughts we dwell,
Finding solace where shadows fell.
Each heartbeat sings an untold song,
In solitude, we find we're strong.

The quiet speaks, a gentle friend,
In the silence, love can mend.
Across the void, we reach and yearn,
In every silence, hearts discern.

With open arms, we greet the night,
In the shadows, find our light.
In solitude, we learn to see,
The beauty in just being free.

So let the world fade into grey,
In the silence, we'll always stay.
For in this space, our souls will bloom,
The language of love dispels the gloom.

Secrets in the Silence

In the void where echoes fade,
Secrets linger, softly laid.
In the hush of twilight's grace,
Hidden dreams find their place.

Between the breaths and fleeting sighs,
Truths emerge, unmasked by lies.
In the silence, whispers start,
Unraveling the tied-up heart.

Every heartbeat tells a tale,
In the quiet, we unveil.
The stories that the night conceals,
In every silence, truth reveals.

With a glance, we share the load,
In the stillness, love bestowed.
Secrets dance when silence sings,
In that space, our heart takes wing.

Do you hear the muted cry?
Hope arises, our spirits fly.
In the silence, always near,
Secrets speak, forever clear.

Unraveled Mysteries

In shadows deep secrets lie,
Whispers echo, truth drawn nigh.
Threads of fate begin to weave,
Unraveled dreams we will believe.

The night conceals the stories told,
In quiet hearts, the past unfolds.
Stars align, a guiding light,
Shattering doubts, igniting flight.

Each corner turned, another clue,
Through veils of fog, we'll push on through.
Unlock the door to realms unknown,
Within the labyrinth, seeds are sown.

Embrace the unknown, take a chance,
In the dance of fate, we advance.
Mysteries tease, they draw us near,
In the search, we conquer fear.

The puzzle's edges start to blend,
In where we start and where we end.
A tapestry of life's embrace,
With every thread, we find our place.

Wind Beneath the Silence

In quiet moments, whispers soar,
A gentle breeze, forever more.
It carries dreams on down the lane,
Through fields untouched by joy or pain.

Though silence reigns, it speaks so loud,
Beneath the stillness, freedom's shroud.
The heartbeats echo, softly chase,
Their cadence shines in empty space.

With every breath, the spirit thrives,
In unseen currents, hope survives.
The wind it knows the paths untold,
In quiet strength, our souls unfold.

Embrace the calm, find solace here,
In whispers close, we shed our fear.
Let silence guide with tender grace,
And rise above life's frantic pace.

To feel the wind, our spirits soar,
It tells of peace forevermore.
In every gust, a promise flows,
That love is where the true heart goes.

Journey Through the Abyss

In darkness deep, the shadows play,
A journey leads through night to day.
With every step, the fear takes hold,
But courage stirs within the cold.

The path may twist, the way may bend,
Through endless night, we find a friend.
In echoes lost, our voices sing,
Emerging strength from suffering.

Stars above like diamonds gleam,
Guiding us through each waking dream.
The abyss whispers, truth be told,
In silence born, our hearts unfold.

Through trials faced, we rise once more,
Each scar a reminder of what's in store.
For in the depths, we shed our skin,
And find the light that dwells within.

A journey vast, yet precious still,
With every dark, a stronger will.
Through the abyss, like shadows blend,
We emerge whole, our spirits mend.

The Unexpressed Longing

In quiet moments, hearts ignite,
A subtle spark veiled from sight.
The unexpressed, a yearning flame,
In shadows deep, it calls our name.

Longing lingers in silent air,
A bittersweet ache, a secret dare.
In muted tones, emotions flow,
A hidden path, where passions grow.

In the depths, the soul does yearn,
For words unspoken, our hearts discern.
A touch, a glance, a fleeting breeze,
In stillness, we find our heart's ease.

Among the stars, our spirits dance,
Yet here we stand, with dreams askance.
The unexpressed calls us to rise,
Embrace the ache, and cut our ties.

For every longing knows its place,
In whispered hope, we find our grace.
Let love ignite what fear concealed,
For in expression, hearts are healed.

Ghosts of Forgotten Dreams

In shadows where memories linger,
Whispers of hopes, softly sing.
Fleeting moments like smoke in the air,
Echoes of joy, now a distant fling.

Chasing reflections that fade into night,
Holding on tight to what once felt so real.
Silent tears fall for the dreams that took flight,
Gone with the dawn, lost in unreal.

Time moves like water, it slips through our hands,
Yet in our hearts, their essence remains.
Ghosts dance in silence on forgotten sands,
Reminders of love, laughter, and pains.

They beckon us gently with fragile grace,
Filling our souls with a muted glow.
Though shadows may gather, we still find our place,
In memories cherished and dreams that still flow.

So let us remember the spark that once shined,
For even in darkness, hope lingers near.
In ghosts of our dreams, we are intertwined,
A tapestry woven of joy and of fear.

Ethereal Pathways

Underneath the silver moonlight,
Wanderers tread on paths unknown.
Dreams weave through the fabric of night,
In twilight's embrace, their journeys are sown.

The stars wink softly, guiding each step,
Whispers of fate swirl in the air.
Eternal travelers, lost in depth,
Finding the light in the shadows we bear.

Branches intertwine like thoughts in our mind,
Rustling gently in the cool night breeze.
Every corner holds secrets we find,
In this realm where time ebbs with ease.

Waves of memories crash on the shore,
Yet hope dances quietly in the mist.
On ethereal pathways, we yearn for more,
Writing our stories that love can't assist.

So follow the glow of your heart's true desire,
Let it consume you, let it ignite.
For in every step, we rise ever higher,
In the haze of the dawn, we will take flight.

The Inner Compass

Within the silence, a voice can be found,
Whispers of truth that guide our way.
Through the chaos, a pulse, a sound,
The inner compass leads us each day.

When shadows cast doubt and fear takes its toll,
Listen closely to the whispers within.
For every lost dream still beckons the soul,
In the heart's quiet chambers, we begin.

Each choice we make shapes the journey we take,
Like ripples that dance on a tranquil lake.
Trust in yourselves when the path seems unclear,
For the compass inside knows no bounds of fear.

With every step forward, feel the embrace,
Of intuitions that surface in time.
They light up the path, revealing our place,
In a world where our spirits can climb.

So heed the direction your heart wants to show,
Inward reflections will help to ignite.
The inner compass leads us to grow,
Illuminating truth in the dark of night.

Unfelt Touches

In the quietest moments, an echo remains,
Of fingers that brushed against love's sweet glow.
Unfelt touches linger, leaving soft stains,
On the canvas of hearts where feelings ought flow.

Just a heartbeat away, yet worlds apart,
The warmth of a glance speaks volumes untold.
Silhouettes dancing can spark the heart,
In the depths of silence, stories unfold.

In unspoken words, emotions reside,
Yearnings and dreams wrapped in fate's gentle hands.
Each moment a treasure, love cannot hide,
As it pulses and weaves through imagined lands.

In shadows entwined, our spirits connect,
Though distance may wane or time drift away.
The unspoken bond grows stronger, erect,
A tapestry woven with care every day.

So cherish the whispers, the glances, the sighs,
For unfelt touches can break down the walls.
In a world of echoes, true love never dies,
It lives in the spaces where the heart calls.

Fables Untold

In shadows deep where secrets lie,
Old tales whisper, passing by.
Creatures dance in moonlit gleam,
Crafting stories, yet unseen.

A fox in red, a raven's call,
Beneath the stars, they spin and crawl.
With every step, a legend grows,
In the forest where no one goes.

Magic lingers in twisted roots,
Reviving dreams that time computes.
Underneath the ancient oaks,
The heart of fables softly pokes.

So heed the tales the night can spin,
For every end hides where we begin.
In every rustle of the leaves,
A story waits, if one believes.

The moon observes with watchful eyes,
While nighttime breathes its lullabies.
In fables told, truths often blend,
A journey taken, no clear end.

The Whispering Woods

Among the trees where silence hums,
A melody of nature drums.
Pine-scented breezes sweep the ground,
In this enchanted place, I'm bound.

Whispers linger on branches thin,
Secrets of the world within.
Softly rustling, they call my name,
A gentle beckoning, a sacred game.

Sunlight dances on leaves above,
Igniting shadows with warmth and love.
In every corner, life takes flight,
The woods alive with pure delight.

Hidden pathways twist and turn,
Every step a new lesson learned.
The heart beats slower, peace unfolds,
In the embrace of stories told.

So listen close, for what is shared,
In whispered winds, we are ensnared.
The woods will speak if you are still,
And fill your spirit with their will.

Beneath the Surface

Delve beneath the calm, clear sea,
Where treasures hide in mystery.
Coral gardens softly sway,
In depths where sunlight fades away.

Creatures glide through liquid dreams,
In shimmering hues and starlit beams.
Echoes of a world unknown,
In silence, wonders are grown.

Rustling sands and hidden caves,
Guard the stories of the brave.
Every current tells a tale,
Of bygone ships, of winds that sail.

Time flows slowly, yet so swift,
Beneath the surface lies the gift.
A realm of peace, of ancient lore,
In the depths, we long to explore.

So plunge into the deep and dark,
Let the ocean leave its mark.
Connect with all that lies below,
For beneath the waves, our spirits grow.

In the Stillness of Night

Under the blanket of endless skies,
Stars twinkle like whispered sighs.
In stillness wrapped, the world holds breath,
In shadows deep, all dreams bequeath.

Moonlight dances on silver streams,
Lighting pathways of forgotten dreams.
A hush prevails, like a fragile plea,
In the calmest hour, we find the key.

Crickets sing their serenade soft,
As the night's embrace lifts us aloft.
Every heartbeat echoes the night,
In solitude, everything feels right.

Thoughts drift like clouds in moonlit air,
Secrets unraveled, a moment rare.
In stillness, we find the way to roam,
For the night calls us softly home.

Embrace the quiet, let worries cease,
In the stillness of night, we find our peace.
With every star, a wish takes flight,
In the hush, we ignite the light.

Soft Steps Through Time's Veil

In shadows deep, we softly tread,
Memories linger where dreams are fed.
A tapestry spun of whispers and sighs,
Time drifts softly, where the past lies.

Each step unveils a forgotten song,
Echoes of love where we once belonged.
With gentle grace, we move along,
In the embrace of a world so strong.

Beneath the stars, the night unfolds,
Stories of hearts, forever told.
In the silent dance of twilight's glow,
Soft steps guide us where rivers flow.

Through misty paths, the journey flows,
Every heartbeat, a tale that grows.
Veils of history, woven tight,
Carry us home through the tranquil night.

So let us wander, hand in hand,
Through the ages of this timeless land.
With soft steps through time's gentle veil,
We'll find our way where love prevails.

A Lament Outside the Noise

In crowded streets, I feel alone,
Voices clamor, yet none are known.
A silent scream within my chest,
Yearning for peace, a place to rest.

The world spins fast, a frantic race,
Faces rush by, devoid of grace.
I search for solace in the din,
A whisper of calm beneath the skin.

Each moment lost in vacant chatter,
Thoughts collide, but none seem to matter.
I seek a pause, a breath, a sigh,
To escape the noise that draws me nigh.

Outside the chaos, I long to be,
Wrapped in the silence, just me and me.
A soft lament, a quiet plea,
Where echoes fade, and I am free.

In the stillness, I find my voice,
In gentle shadows, I make my choice.
To rise above the pounding sound,
And let my spirit break the ground.

The Calm Before Discovery

Before the dawn, a hush prevails,
A secret whisper in the gales.
Collecting thoughts as night departs,
A canvas blank for eager hearts.

The pause before the journey starts,
The stillness hums with hopeful arts.
In quiet moments, dreams ignite,
Shimmering softly through the night.

When clouds part ways, and light breaks through,
A world unknown, wake up anew.
Each heartbeat quickens, breaths align,
In the calm before the stars combine.

Curiosity, a steady flame,
Fuels the spirit, sparks the brain.
With every sigh, the future calls,
In silence, wisdom gently sprawls.

So let us pause, embrace the wait,
For soon the winds will shift our fate.
In the calm that crowns the dawn's birth,
We find our place upon the Earth.

Navigating the Whispering Woods

Through branches low, the shadows play,
Whispering secrets of the day.
Footfalls soft on a leaf-strewn trail,
Guided by stories that softly sail.

The rustling leaves share tales untold,
Of ancient paths and hearts of gold.
Echoes linger where the wild things roam,
In the woods, we find our home.

Each twist and turn, a mystery hides,
Nature's voice in the gentle tides.
The heartbeats of creatures, near and far,
Lead us onward, like a distant star.

Among the trees, a solace found,
In the quiet, the world slows down.
With every step, a bond we weave,
Part of the forest, we dare believe.

So let us wander where whispers flow,
In the woods, where time moves slow.
With open hearts and eyes that see,
Navigating the dream of what can be.

The Path of Unspoken Dreams

Beneath the stars, our wishes lie,
Whispers float like clouds on high.
With every stride, the silence grows,
Unseen paths where longing flows.

In shadows deep, the heart takes flight,
Chasing echoes throughout the night.
Invisible threads, the soul's embrace,
In realms of hope, we find our place.

A journey marked by unseen signs,
In the depths where courage shines.
Embers glow in the darkened seams,
For we walk the path of dreams.

Time drifts softly, like a sigh,
As we chase the moments nigh.
Each step forward, a silent plea,
To awaken what wishes will be.

With every breath, the night unfolds,
The story of dreams, quietly told.
Together we chase what lies ahead,
On this path, where we dare to tread.

Veil of the Unheard

Behind the noise, a silence waits,
Wrapped in layers, bound by fates.
Unspoken words dance in the mist,
What's lost to time, still can't be missed.

In shadows cast, the whispers creep,
A melody that stirs the deep.
Voices echo through the haze,
Lost in the labyrinth of our days.

A heart that beats beneath the pain,
Yearns to speak, but stays in vain.
The veil conceals what wants to shine,
A world where the unspoken twines.

Cradled soft in twilight's fold,
Secrets lie like dreams of old.
With every breath, the longing grows,
In the stillness, the heart knows.

So let us find the hidden sound,
In the silence where truth is found.
Beyond the veil, the soul takes flight,
Yearning for the day from night.

Solitary Shadows

In the hush, the shadows play,
Waltzing slowly, fading away.
Each figure holds a tale to tell,
Of whispered thoughts cast under spell.

Lonely corners, a silent sigh,
Flickering dreams as time drifts by.
In solitude's embrace we find,
A mirror reflecting the heart's mind.

With every dusk, the shadows blend,
Where solitude becomes a friend.
A quiet pulse, a gentle moral,
In the dark, we hear our oral.

Moments linger, a quiet space,
As shadows dance with tender grace.
Lost in thoughts, they intertwine,
In the ether where stars align.

Together they build a tale anew,
In shades of grey, they find their hue.
In solitude, we come to know,
The depth of shadows' gentle flow.

In Search of the Quiet Light

Through valleys low, we wander wide,
In search of hope, our hearts abide.
Guided by stars that softly gleam,
Awakening the soul's own dream.

Across the night, with tender grace,
We tread the path in quiet space.
Where shadows blend and whispers sigh,
In this realm, we learn to fly.

The gentle glow, a beacon bright,
Illuminates the darkest night.
Every flicker, a ray of trust,
A dance of faith in the quiet dust.

With every step, we seek the flame,
A flickering heart without a name.
In the stillness, we find our sight,
In pursuit of that quiet light.

From chaos born, a calm takes form,
Where dreams are held and hearts transform.
With open arms, we greet the dawn,
In search of light, we journey on.

www.ingramcontent.com/pod-product-compliance
Ingram Content Group UK Ltd.
Pitfield, Milton Keynes, MK11 3LW, UK
UKHW021302280125
4330UKWH00005B/91